Everything Is Radiant
Between the Hates

Everything Is Radiant Between the Hates

poems

Rich Ferguson

MOON
TIDE PRESS

~ 2021 ~

Meg –
Keep On
Being
the
Bright Light
You Are
Shine On
♡ Rich

Everything Is Radiant Between the Hates

Editor-in-chief
Eric Morago

Associate Editor
José Enrique Medina

Editor Emeritus
Michael Miller

Marketing Director
Dania Alkhouli

Marketing Assistant
Ellen Webre

Proofreader
Jim Hoggatt

Front cover art
Joanna C. Valente

Author photo
Alexis Rhone Fancher

Book design
Michael Wada

Moon Tide logo design
Abraham Gomez

Everything Is Radiant Between the Hates
is published by Moon Tide Press

Moon Tide Press
6709 Washington Ave. #9297, Whittier, CA 90608
www.moontidepress.com

FIRST EDITION

Printed in the United States of America

ISBN # 978-1-7350378-2-0

Further Praise for
Everything Is Radiant Between the Hates...

Rich Ferguson's work never fails to thrill readers while deeply touching their minds and souls. We need writers like this. We need books like this.

— Rob Roberge, author of *The Cost of Living*, and
Working Backwards from the Worst Moment of My Life

Everything Is Radiant Between the Hates is a superb and timely collection from a poet who puts the "artist" in "spoken-word artist."

— Greg Olear, author of *FATHERMUCKER* and *TOTALLY KILLER*

Rich Ferguson's poetry is open, generous, silly, subversive and, at its core, hopeful.

— Kim Shuck, 7th Poet Laureate of San Francisco,
author of *Deer Trails* and *Whose Water?*

Pulsing with a passion for language, *Everything Is Radiant Between the Hates* also displays a yearning for renewal and a demand for justice. This is essential poetry.

— Jane Ormerod, writer, performer, and publisher

Rich Ferguson's *Everything Is Radiant Between the Hates* shows the remarkable range of his poetry: vivid, moving, and profound.

— Richard Modiano, Executive Director Emeritus
Beyond Baroque Foundation

The only thing more exciting than experiencing Rich Ferguson's genius in person is to savor his explosive words on the page.

— Alexis Rhone Fancher, author of Junkie Wife and
poetry editor of *Cultural Weekly*

Both elegant of need and prosaic of necessity, this poetry is an activism of the heart, as it states with almost offhand eloquence, "All love shall go unhushed." Let it be so.

— Richard Loranger, author of *Sudden Windows* and *Poems for Teeth*

Ferguson drums on the dashboard in revelatory beats, driving, guiding us through the Southland, our benighted republic, and beyond.

— Andrew Tonkovich, author of *The Dairy of Anne Frank*, host of *Bibliocracy Radio*

Ferguson is a singular voice of our community, an honest and generous teller of vivid stories of our benighted, betrayed and still somehow beautiful city.

— Lisa Alvarez, editor of the forthcoming poetry anthology, *Why to These Rocks: 50 Years of Poems from the Community of Writers* (Heyday 2021) with foreword by Robert Hass

Never before has self-liberation within a heartfelt community felt so inviting, as well as so surprisingly accessible.

— Bill Mohr, Ph.D., author of *Holdouts, The Los Angeles Poetry Renaissance 1948-1992*

Rich Ferguson could probably write better things in his sleep than most people can in their waking hours. This Los Angeles writer is truly a gifted and talented force to recognized and cherished.

— Iris Berry, author of *All That Shines Under the Hollywood Sign*, editor at Punk Hostage Press

Rich Ferguson is a word contortionist, bending language that at once reveals atrocity while instilling hope.

— Susan Hayden, creator of *Library Girl*

A glorious celebration of language glowing with the exuberant joy of a poet possessed by the muse, Rich Ferguson's *Radiant* is an unapologetic love affair with the word.

— S.A. Griffin, author of *Dreams Gone Mad with Hope* and *The Fire is Ours*. Editor, *The Outlaw Bible of American Poetry*

For Evelyn Everything

Contents

THE GYM BEYOND GOOD AND EVIL TENDENCIES

EVERYTHING IS RADIANT BETWEEN THE HATES

IN MY CITY OF WORDS

AN ABRIDGED HISTORY OF LIPS

EVELYN EVERYTHING

Foreword

Rich Ferguson doesn't look away. He holds the line. With every poem, he puts his body on the line. And in the line. The line is around his body.

First, to the body of work: it is a heroic body. Eight sections of poems, in many keys, on vastly different subjects, the scope of experience charted likewise varied; big griefs, explosive desires, hollows of absence that approach the abysmal; thoughts and imagery composed of small chuckles, of tiny mending bird bones, and on down to the molecules, the DNA of mistakes that cannot be remedied but, is it possible, with spit, polish and intake of breath, can be altered?

The masculine body of the 21st century is a contested and wounded body. To attempt heroism is again noble and not reactionary because the reactionaries no longer pretend: they are openly confidence men, wearing ugly red hats and entertaining themselves with the gladiatorial glee of seeing detained refugee children fed alive to the ravages of Covid as they shop in Rich's poem, at the "MAGA Mall of America."

Like Orwell's *Down and Out in Paris & London*, the working man's body is etched on Ferguson's page: "…out of the deep, ragged pocket of society's worn-down blues, /countless citizens dancing to the up-tempo /of the down-low." The very act of writing after a long day's work, is a subliminal chorus running like a chain link under his (dearly-won) free verse.

And though Ferguson may roam the same billboarded and tattoo-parlored boulevards that Fante and Bukowski once traveled, he sees with very different eyes and aim. There is a reason a gabillion middle-aged woman are crazy about *Outlander* and *Poldark* and perhaps, unexpectedly, that has some relation to why this poetry speaks powerfully to this moment. In both can be discovered the revival of a valiant kind of masculinity, yes, but it's not about a "make men great again" nostalgia. It is about what the 21st century does to that male body. What marriage does, what fatherhood does, what the job does, the drive home on the freeway does, what memory does, what age does, what youth was. How hard is it to keep working for six-pack abs in "The Gym beyond Good and Evil?" What do mass killings do to your soul and what arguments can you have with a body politic which is politically illiterate and projecting a mass mirage? (*Autopsy Of Democracy*).

We are in a battle between perceived good and perceived evil, between felt love and felt hatred. And Rich's passionate and resolutely un-postmodern body of work within these pages as well as his physical body as a vessel, vehicle and sacrificial knight of his poetic craft is prime for this epochal struggle.

The poems you are about to absorb hold the stare of these ugly days without succumbing to either the ugliness, or the despair at the ugli-ness. The biggest hopes of humanity and the smallest hairs of moments bend to this poet's project. But not to his will, though his stubbornness is evident in every stone he drags to his circle of sacred observance; No, the bending of little and great, trivial and crucial is not achieved through will. Rather it is a simple experiment, a hypothesis lived out daily: What if, he asks, we continue to love?

— Heather Woodbury

More and more, it seems our errand is to face the music, bring the noise, scour the rocks to salvage grace notes and fragmented harmonies, diving for pearls in the beautiful ruins...

— Campbell McGrath

The world has tired of tears. We weep owls now. They live longer. They know their way in the dark.

— Natalie Diaz

Once Upon a Many Sleepless Nights

I study the dental records
of long-forgotten moons.

Write eulogies
for lost socks.

Play first trombone
in the coyote orchestra.

I collaborate with clouds,
creating poems
continuously changing
shape & meaning,
depending upon
how you look at them.

Worry Beads
and
Blessings

A Worry Bead, a Blessing

From the deep blues
of my mother's belly
I wailed my way
to birth-light.

Was branded
with a name
passed down
through ten generations
of midnight.

My mother cradled me
in her arms,
whispered in my ear.

She told me
I'd been born
into a world
of bombs & birdsongs,
saints & slaughterhouses,
shackles & happy hours.

My mother said
we humans are
the bold electricity of kisses,
and screams
stuffed with
the latest headlines.

We are
correctly tied shoelaces
and rusted hinges.
Healed wounds
and broken mirrors.

She
wrung ten sad songs
from the ghost in me,
then handed me over
to a brass-knuckled moon.
It pummeled me to sleep
with a busted-lip lullaby.

In dreamland,
I didn't count fleeting sheep,
just heavy bruises.

As I grew,
optimism became a consequence
of my wishbone ribcage.

Some days,
those ribs have broken
to the side of good fortune.
Other times,
I've been left wailing
my birth-given blues.

Nightly,
I shed my weighty shadow
beneath a hanging tree.
Nightly,
I count the stars
in the night sky.

Each one: a worry bead.
Each one: a blessing.

When Called in For Questioning

When asked about the scars around your lips, tell them you were speaking peace in a shattered-glass world. When asked about employment, say you are a wound collector on the broken frontier. As for where you reside, tell them your heart is equidistant from joy & suffering, the now & never, the sweet flower & the Hiroshima cloud. Regarding why you say the things you say, tell them the full moon is in your mouth. When asked about the ghosts behind your eyes, say you occasionally spend too much time thinking about who you are to become, rather than whom you are supposed to be. As for why some leave the world too soon, tell them death's reflexes are occasionally quicker than prayer.

What My Inner Executioner Has Told Me On Many Sleepless Nights

No blindfold,
no last cigarette,
no last words,
no last meal:
self-doubt's firing squad
shows no mercy.

Phantom Poem Syndrome
for Joel Landmine

it's the unspoken words
lying fallow on the tongue.

it's the ghostly limb
sprouting from the heart;
shadow & vacuity
its new flesh & bone.

it's the things you can't quite reach—
the off switch on your fear machine,
or the gratitude grenade
to obliterate discontent.

it's everything in your brain,
restless & raging;
a chainsaw with A.D.D.

it's the suicidal tendencies
moving at terminal velocity.

it's the gun
that can't stop jonesing
for a wild & hating hand
to keep its barrel warm at night.

Chalk Liveforever (*Dudleya pulverulenta*)

for Anne Yale

Sweet is your suffering,
you vector for foliage-annihilating viruses—

you wayward home
for slugs and mealybugs.

Perhaps
it is your graceful acceptance of pain
allowing you to endure dry summer habitats,

and to persist for months when uprooted from soil.

Fall and winter rains reawaken you
from drought-wracked dormancy.

Nature coronates you, spike-crowned,
tufted colony keeper;

resilient bearer of solitary rosette;
dizzy dazzler of leaf shapes and sizes.

Your name *Liveforever*
speaks to your ability to feed on neglect,
create your flowering.

Just Moments After Eternity's Musicians Had Taken a Break to Retune Their Instruments

after Kimberly Brooks' Hall of Eternity

I recall,
a long, silent hallway;
a gracious home
leaning towards the lips
of tranquility—

a soon-to-be kiss
yearning to be
memorialized by elegance,
framed by hands
cut off from
the elbows of war.

Just outside
the front door—

pills of hate
swallowed by the bitter masses;
drugged and wailing shards
of amnesiac moonlight
preying upon hopeless lovers;
reason sleepwalking
into the wide-open mouths
of guns.

Those left alive and unscathed
tattoo their memories
with shadows, nightmares, rubble.

A way to remember
what they no longer wish to.

When Her Blood-Red Kiss Stains My Breath

She is an amnesiac moon,
a lunatic laundromat
robbing me of my quarters.

She possesses
tombstone tarot cards;
ties my pulse
into a hangman's knot.

She is a forever leaving ship;
my arms ache
from perpetually waving goodbye.

A nightmare
strapped to a boomerang;
the rush of blood before the injury,
the jagged scar preceding the wound.

She tells me
the knife
she's plunged into my back
will only be there temporarily,
as long as it takes
to find someone else
to carry it for her.

In the center of my chest,
she builds a church
of the disassembled—
a mangled and bloody-faced gospel
bombed on unholy water,
tearing me apart
one heartbeat at a time.

She tells me,
this is how she loves me.

She tells me
whatever I do
with my very next breath,
don't say no.

He Says, She Says

He says, what does this mean?

She says, it means what it feels like it means.

He says, but I don't feel anything.

She says, that could mean everything.

He says, but what if we play the record backwards?
What if we hold our memories up to a mirror?
What will they see that we don't?

She says, the flowers I once picked for you are now wild dogs snarling at the door.

He says, I'll build a new house whose location is known only to us.

She says, our bed is a graveyard.

He says, those snarling dogs at the door, I've turned them back into flowers and have placed them by your pillow.

She says, your spider logic has eight legs too many on which to offer any truth.

He says, I'll write us a new life if only I can find a pen that uses my blood for ink.

She says, you're like the hangover I haven't suffered in years.

He says, you're the empty bottle from which I find it difficult to consume a moment's peace.

She says, your hands are wounded birds I once thought I could heal.

He says, these aren't birds, these hands are restless musical notes
still   searching out their song.

She says, the moon is the moon is the moon.

He says, the moon is the bittersweet symphony I used to sing to you on summer nights.

She says, last night I dreamed you got lost in a desert of your bleached-bone sorrow.

He says, did I make it out alive before your alarm clock went off?

She says nothing.

He says, funny how a silence can say everything.

She says,   distance is the best medicine for us.

He says, I'll leave my shadow by the door in case you change your mind.

She says, roll over and go to sleep.

He says, I've been rolling in my grave for lifetimes.

She says, why did we even get together in the first place?

He says, life's answers are interesting when one only has lightning to read by.

She says, it's cold outside.

He says, the wind now

c
  a
    r
      r
       i
         e
          s

              the shape of who we are.

She says, these days with you are gifts I no longer wish to receive.

He says, I never know what shirt fits me best when I wear
my heart on my sleeve.

She says, don't worry. The heart maintains its beat even

when its love moves on.

certain days feel so heavy

like that final weight pallbearers carry to the grave.
yet say the correct password,

and the moon will allow you into its secret room
behind the shine.

that's where good luck wears the scent
of new laundry behind its ears,

where our brightest essence illuminates dark waters.

the clock tells me when it claps its hands,
i can open my eyes.

it's then i'll be older than i remember,
and younger than i care to forget.

should you see me holding something to the light,
it's a letter i meant to send you

before all these troubles left their shadows at our door.

Not on Your Grave

The most joyful moment of the tale is when the woman says to the man, I will dance with you now, not on your grave. The most joyful moment of the song is when the melody hymns to the listener, I will dance with you now, not on your grave. The stranger standing in the shadows who seems to be wielding a gun but is really a heart on his sleeve as he says, I will dance with you now, not on your grave. The most joyful moment is when the child says it to a parent. When the moon croons it to the tired and lonely driver. When all our ghosts, bundled in the flesh of the moment, reach for our hand and offer: teach us how to dance.

What Was Said at the Reunion of Deathbed Wishes

I wanna seek out tomorrows that drink optimism
   straight no chaser

I wanna dress our deepest sorrows in easy-to-shed miseries.

Wanna remove all billboards from the overcrowded highways in our
minds.

I wanna prove that white noise loves black jazz.

That Mr. Rogers was a CIA operative hired to test the limits of
human kindness.

That the reason dogs howl is because it's far easier than reciting
Ginsberg's
   "Howl" by memory.

I wanna create drive-thru therapy for when we just need a to-go cup
of healing.

Build monuments to love letters still written by hand.

Offer landmark status to all remaining phone booths.

I wanna construct bookstores on Mars, underground libraries for
bookworms.

Create playgrounds in the cloudy eyes of the dying.

I wanna expose all false idols for being truly idle.

Recycle old lies into lions guarding the gates of greatness.

Wanna televise the next revolution without any commercials.

Create a medication to remove all self-inflicted blemishes from our conscience.

I wanna drop poetry bombs into lives without enlightenment.

Compose songs of tectonic forgiveness along all our faults.

I wanna swap eyes with a stranger to see how others witness life.

One With the World, One With Yourself

Be one with the tranquility gallery
behind your eyes,
its humble paintings
of peace and prosperity.
One with how that gallery
is so often under reconstruction, deconstruction.
One with how everything
is so impermanent, so fleeting.
How your every thought
breeds Frankensteins and angels.
Be one with all your Frankensteins and angels.

Be one with being wide-awake,
with everyday magic,
the abracadabra of glorious allegory
written into your every step.
Be one with the forward and backward
of all your human steps:
how in every positive action,
seeds of limitation find their way to fruition.
Be one with the bitter fruit
of not always getting what you want.
May that bitterness
help your successes taste all the sweeter.

Be one with money:
clean money, blood money, funny money.
One with the hard work
you offer as daily sacrifice to the nine-to-five grind.
One with all the con artists, sham shamans,
and common thugs:
all those constantly wanting
to take a bite out of your wallet,
your pocketbook,
your higher consciousness, and life.

Be one with these terrorist times:
how glittering guns
are the new silver spoon given to newborns,
how bombs can be so readily made
from common household products;
strapped to the waists of suicide junkies
or packed into vehicles and driven to your doorstep.
Be one with the song of napalm encoded into your DNA,
the inherent and self-annihilating dirge
of burn, baby, burn.

Be one with our climate changing,
severe weather patterns
of hurricanes, blinding heat,
polar ice caps melting into water,
so much water.
Be one with water. All waters:
flood waters, baptismal waters,
life-giving, life-taking waters.
Be one with how something
so clean and pure as water
can be both womb and tomb.

Be one with being somebody, nobody.
One with how you can write your name
ten thousand times across the chalkboard sky,
yet still never claim the heavens as your own.
Better to share the sun, moon and stars.
Better to see your lover's face
when you stare deeply into the cosmic mirror.

Be one with society's crazy diamonds:
the lost souls, lunatics,
restless romantics and the like.
One with how you all yearn to shine so bright.
How you thread flesh and blood through durable needles, sewing
yourselves into the fabric of life,
staying close to the lines of reality,
but often straying to dream.

Be one with your inner child,
and all the paper airplanes he or she creates.
Be one with your inner TSA agent
when he wants to check your emotional baggage
and perform cavity searches
before you board those paper airplanes
taking off on great flights of imagination.
Know your inner TSA agent's ultimate job
is to ensure safe travel.
But also know that sometimes the safest flights
aren't always the best.
Be one with your inner TSA agent.
One with your inner child and all the paper airplanes.
Be one with the sailing away.

Be one with traveling
down your inner and outer highways,
one with the treasures they may reveal along the way.
Be one with traffic,
the slow drivers and road-rage drivers.
One with your city's boozers and beauties,
the deities and needy,
lost souls and restless romantics
dancing beneath a peroxide-blonde moon,
accompanied by the music
of mockingbirds and apocalypse jukeboxes
as coyote radar surfs the airwaves,
searching out the perfect thrill, the perfect kill
penned in blood
and written across the first and last breath of all things.
Be one with the first and last breath of all things.

Be one with the tic-toc-ticking of the clock.
The hands of time holding you for only a moment,
then moving on.
Be one with how no moment in time
shall ever be repeated the same way twice.
One with how you are a different person
from one moment to the next:
you slough dead skin cells; dead hair;
fingernails and toenails growing;

thoughts changing;
the molecular structures creating you,
both living and dying at the same time.

Be one with how your body and being
will eventually fail you.
One with the day when you'll become a stranger
to everyone and yourself.
Be one with death:
death of family, friends, loved ones.
Pet death. Great big overwhelming universe death.
Be one with the final, everlasting great Big Bang of it all.

Be one with the grass on your future grave.
May it be filled with a million volts
of goodness and green.
May it offer a home to insects and other wildlife.
May it welcome and bear the weight
of those who pass over you.
May the grass on your future grave
be drunk on sunspeak and rise-n-shine.
May it witness the world with eyes of all-seeing bright.
May it pray to the saint of rain.

Be one with the world, one with yourself.
One with the rich man
with slums running through his veins,
one with the beggar possessing a cathedral heart.

Be one
with your Frankensteins and angels,
the boozers and beauties,
deities and needy.
Lost souls, restless romantics,
Republicans and Democrats,
sham shamans and bombs,
hurricanes and pain,
be one with the tic-toc-ticking
of the great Big Bang-of-it-all clock.

Send them all
loving and luminous messages
through the dark and dead of night,
typed on the telegraph keys of your heart.

In the Gomorrah
of Glamour and
Gimme All You Can

In the Gomorrah of Glamour
and Gimme All You Can
for Wanda Coleman

Life is
one long madness
in the
Gomorrah of Glamour
and
Gimme All You Can.

We,
the living,
wander between
absolute truths
and the delusions
of cap-teethed,
vacant-eyed madonnas
flashing fistfuls
of nirvanaless dollars.

Ballistic spiritualists
and
CIA operatives
disguised as holy prophets
stand on street corners,
shouting machinated missives;

a perpetuation
of purposeless paranoia
and pointless
preambles of pandemonium;

while
media-hungry whores—
whose body temples
have been desecrated
by gods of addiction—

trick their souls
for another toke
off the cash pipe:

one suck
can bring
15 minutes of fame,
or a
sudden OD on vanity.

Life is
one long crash and burn
in the
Gomorrah of Glamour
and
Gimme All You Can.

Our
aggressions,
obsessions,
denials and denigrations
build the cornerstone
of planned obsolescence;

crying out to the world,
expecting echoes
of salvation,
receiving only
long, unforgivable silences;

trying
to shake off
all the insults
and innuendos
nailed to our bones;

bellyfuls of
brutalities and betrayals
acquired over a lifetime,

fattened up on fatalism,
while myopic optimism
stumbles blindly
down the boulevard
of extremely bad behavior;

where
rapists, tailgaters,
drug pushers, pedophiles,
stalkers, shit talkers,
insomniacs,
crash addicts
and detritus riders
on the storm
of prefabricated love—
suffering the PTSD
of junkyard LSD—
rain down disease and need

on a
saviorless
City of Angels
where
buried underground
one can find more
serial-killer corpses
than new sources of water—

sometimes
the only thing
that can quench
the thirst
is bloodlust.

Life is
one long sadness
in the
Gomorrah of Glamour
and
Gimme All You Can.

Not even tigers
can guard
this landscape of fading ease.
What were once wings
are now only
clipped eclipses
in fancy clothes.

No sympathy
or healing tea-leaf readings;
only barbed wire
and indignation,

as
pain and suffering
slip through the cracks
like smoke;
cloud mirrors
that can no longer
look us in the eye.

So quarrelsome
are these days
packing
brass-knuckled troubles;

jacked up
on limited visions
of what were once
so brightly promised tomorrows,

while in defense
we
stand armed
with only aerosol cans
of "I Think I Can"
downgraded to:

"No How, No Way."

Every moment,
the future
looks dimmer.

Life is cheap.

As for death:

if,
by chance,
there's rebirth,

it will only be available
to witness
on a limited basis
through pay-per-view.

Another Day in L.A.

1.

Early morning symphony
of coffee brewing, babies burbling,
truck gears grinding, industry wheezing.
Blackbirds singing,
barrio bus-stop benches creaking,
emaciated mop-top rock-star palm trees
rustling in the breeze.

Those unheard:
the sleeping, the dead,
and stealthy coyotes
lurking through Los Feliz neighborhoods,
hunting down
garbage scraps and stray pets.

2.

Bankers, lawyers, gangbangers.
Homemakers, social workers, sexworkers.
Everyone making deals:
another fix, another fuck, another driveby.
Another marriage abolished or saved.
Deals being made in high-rises, hotel rooms,
parked cars, courtrooms, kitchens.
Sleazy deals tattooed with diamonds and dollar signs.
Honorable deals sealed with a handshake.
Desperate deals gone so wrong,
not even the shadows stick around to witness
all the dark that went down.

3.

From Hollywood to Hawthorne,
Watts to Woodland Hills:
the circling and buzzing of police helicopters.

Urban birds singing only the blues.

4.

People rushing to jobs, gyms,
malls, AA meetings.
Everyone searching for, or escaping:
demons, death, money, love, salvation.
Hurry.
It's only seconds
before someone pulls a trigger.
Only seconds
before someone plants the seeds
of a kiss.

5.

Promises flimsy as negligees.
Dreams too big
for a million hearts to hold.
Become a star
or slip through the cracks,
dwell anonymously as dust.
That aching feeling deep inside:
an eviction notice
being posted on your soul.

6.

Car exhaust, factory pollution,
byproducts from aerosol cans,
and wildfire smoke
crowd out the sky.
Skull-and-crossbones breathing,
noxious and obnoxious breathing.
At least some are comforted by the notion
that all the poisons
make for beautiful sunsets.

7.

Evening injects meth,
makes once-wished-upon stars edgy,
chronically reaching for the burned-spoon moon.
Beneath tweaked-out galaxies,
people struggle for direction, meaning.
Others craving more faithful
and comforting constellations
visit the walk-of-fame stars
on Hollywood Boulevard.

8.

Bars that are more like churches,
streethustlers that are more like healers.
Here,
lives can be lost and saved
in many ways.

9.

The dutiful and the damned,
the famous and freakish.
Clergy members,
counterfeiters, cancer patients:
all are blessed and unified in slumber.

But once the bedside alarm rings,
it's half past one's own version
of heaven or hell.

Wanting

Dustballs want to be bullet trains.
Bullet trains want to be snails.
Snails want to be crows.
Crows want to be Beethoven's Fifth.
Beethoven's Fifth wants to be a fifth of gin.
A fifth of gin wants to be holy water.
Holy water wants to be mud puddles.
Mud puddles want to be rainbows.
Rainbows want to be nooses.
Nooses want to be church bells.
Church bells want to be bongs.
Bongs want to be butterflies.
Butterflies want to be buffalo stampedes.
Buffalo stampedes want to be angels dancing on the head
    of a pin.
Angels dancing on the head of a pin want to be solar
    systems swirling.
Solar systems swirling want to be sandboxes.
Sandboxes want to be mountains.
Mountains want to be ladybugs.
Ladybugs want to be wolves.
Wolves want to be radios.
Radios want to be moments of silence.
Moments of silence want to be lightning and thunder.
Lightning and thunder want to be serial killers.
Serial killers want to be reborn into baby Buddhas.
Baby Buddhas want to grow up to be electric guitars.
Electric guitars want to be junkyard dogs.
Junkyard dogs want to be anything but a cat.
A cat wants to be a Cadillac.
A Cadillac wants to be a garbage truck.
A garbage truck wants to be a wet dream.
A wet dream wants to be heaven.
Heaven wants to be a dive bar.
A dive bar wants to be diamonds.
Diamonds want to be handfuls of dirt.
Handfuls of dirt want to be thrown into graves.
Graves want to be winds.
Winds want to be human.

And humans are forever wanting
to be
everything
at once.

Why I Can't Keep the Days of the Week Straight

Mondays feel more like Sundays
crossdressing as Fridays
on a hot-date Saturday night

Deep in the Bowels of a One-Note Downtown
for Bob Kaufman

The fire hydrant is teaching the local Girl Scouts' Club
how to pee while standing up.
I have a crush on a buffalo on the back of a hard-to-find
1937 nickel.
My downstairs neighbor is fluent in pain-in-the-ass
& I only speak a little nightingale.

The fire hydrant is teaching the local Girl Scouts' Club
how to pee while standing up.
PG&E is threatening to shut off my tears
& grave robbers keep digging up
my old fantasies, threatening to sell them on eBay.

I once crashed a party in my own imagination,
only to be thrown out
for not being able to conduct a coherent conversation
with myself.
I squeezed my brain
into a Victoria's Secret black push-up bra,
but it did nothing to enhance my sexual
or intellectual capacity.

The local Girl Scouts are teaching the fire hydrant
how to build confidence & character.
The buffalo I had a crush on, on the back of a hard-to-find 1937
nickel
has now become extinct.
My downstairs neighbor has murdered my nightingales.

The local Girl Scouts are teaching the fire hydrant
how to build confidence & character.
My old fantasies have been cobbled into tombstone shoes.
All my tears are drying out in a prison cell in a town called You're
Fuck Outta Luck.
My downstairs neighbor is the jailer.

If you want to call a lost loved one in the afterlife,
it should be noted that ghosts have difficulties
picking up phones.

If you want to send me a love letter by echo,
it probably won't arrive
until long after my inner child is dead and gone.

That's the trick
with living so deep in the bowels
of a one-note downtown—

the only thing you can rely upon
is the continual cry of sirens.

Soundtrack to a Modern-Day L.A. Palm Noir

Sounds of
Hollywoodland thrills and chills
set in ultra-moody hues
of 1940s and 50s gangster L.A.—

brass-knuckled fast talk
of hardboiled thugs and detectives;
kiss-me-deadly melodies
of femme fatales;
bar brawls, cat calls;
the cold click
of stiletto heels, stiletto blades,
and morgue cooler doors
closing on still another John Doe.

Those sounds mixed
with present-day sounds—

riotous rhythms
forged from hands
of Leimert Park djembe demigods
break-beating on wings
of rap and revolution.

Car horns, car radios, car alarms.

Freeways clogged
with huddled and befuddled masses
inching towards
invention, reinvention,
prosperity, invisibility.

The bark and bite
of bulldogs and bulldog revolvers.

Our past and present city sounds,
combining and recombining
to create the soundtrack
to a modern-day L.A. palm noir—

a white heat,
double indemnity,
song of live and die
set deep in the blood,
pulsing through the hearts and minds
of one and all:

Century City lawyers
to San Pedro dockworkers;
Westside yoga warriors
to Skid Row worriers;
drug addicts to the clean and sober;
clergy members to tattooed rock gods;
those on their deathbeds,
and those suffering
from fever dreams of almighty stardom.

Our soundtrack
to a modern-day L.A. palm noir—

packs
the hot and howling will
of Santa Ana winds;
earworms its way into our souls,
jukeboxes with our inner demons.

Seeks alleyways
as if they're confessionals
in which to share sins.

It's
mirrors and reflections,
rain and complex plotlines.

Fingernails
dragging across
our blackboard jungle brains
as that voice in our head proclaims:

"Yeah,
I'm beaten up,
but I'm not beaten…
and I'm not quittin'."

Our soundtrack
to a modern-day L.A. palm noir—

stained with a history
of its notorious crimes
and criminals:

from the Black Dahlia,
to Sharon Tate,
the Hillside Stranger,
to the Grim Sleeper.

It's a hymn
filled with
hums of late-night neon signs,
and the short vowel sound
of death's last sigh
on a victim's lips.

Oms and bad omens,
sirens and babies crying.

Police helicopters
circling, buzzing
like hornets
out for a sudden sting.

One must develop an ear
for our city song;
harmonize slow and steady
at first
then cruise
into the fast lane;

dodge multi-car pileups
of those who've burned out
before burning bright;
anxious leaps of faith
that only a precious few
have survived.

Our soundtrack
to a modern-day L.A. palm noir—

a lurid and lethal hunger
fueled by gasoline, sweat, and tears.

Decked out
in false eyelashes,
and false promises;
it's a true love and true crime booty call
wooing with stroked and stoked hallelujahs
purring like sex kittens
knitting kisses out of thin air.

Moving, grooving,
coaxing, cajoling,
ready to find us
innocent or guilty
beneath midnight streetlights
shining like halos and interrogation lights.

Our soundtrack
to a modern-day L.A. palm noir—

it's a death song
in the key of cordite
heard by Sam Cooke
when taking a bullet
at the Hacienda Hotel.

It's a non-stop party song
wailed by Tom Waits, Iggy Pop, and Janis Joplin
at the Tropicana
in the low-rent, high-spirited late 60s.

Songbirds sit on phonelines
mimicking our city's
rev and dread soundtrack.

Earthquakes only visit us
'cause they wanna learn
how to shake, rattle, and roll
like we do.

From Olivera Street to Rodeo Drive,
from Watts Tower to the Miracle Mile—

generations of races and ethnicities,
occupations and preoccupations
adding to our city song:

from labor movements
battling 1920s union busters,
to 50s and 60s Chavez Ravine families
facing down bulldozers and eviction notices;

from African Americans
chased out of 1930s sundown towns,
to the later cries of Rodney King
when suffering the blows and bruises
of racism-wielding police;

from the Technicolor visions of Timothy Leary
to the Technikiller machinations of Raymond Chandler.

Our city song,
it can be so serious and surreal—

drum loops of dull footsteps
pacing confines
of 6-by-8 cells
at Men's Central Jail,
mixed with the disembodied voice
of Joe Gillis narrating the story
of Sunset Boulevard
while floating dead in a swimming pool.

Other days,
our city song
is a raucous hip hop
krumping and locking
down Hollywood Boulevard;

a funky, freestyle
red-carpet gala
popping with paparazzi
and klieg-light bonfires
illuminating our highest selves—

let us shine,
let us shine,
let us shine.

Our gangsterfied and glorified
city sounds
revving their engines,
burning rubber on asphalt,
breaking all natural and supernatural speed limits;
drag-racing down the 10 Freeway,
the 5, 405, 101, and 60
to all points
North, South, East, West.

From Koreatown to Croatian Place,
Little Moscow to Little Ethiopia,
Lake Balboa to Larchmont,
Echo Park to the Palisades.

Every shade
in L.A.'s urban crayon box
creating
the mood, mystery,
shadows and light
harboring the living and dead,
everything existing
between celluloid and the flesh;

all the devils and angels
that are our dance partners
in this manic and mystical,
sadistic and symphonic soundtrack
to our modern-day L.A. palm noir.

The Autopsy of Democracy

Single Maligned Female

Maligned, misappropriated, torch-bearing woman seeks a loving relationship with a free-minded country, including all its tired, poor, and huddled immigrant masses. Must be benevolent, enlightened, and able to relocate to New York City area. Willing to overlook baldness, impotency, and certain STDs so long as you're not an oppressive, egomaniacal tyrant, and are into plus-sized, copper-skinned women. Open to ethnic origin, religion, and sexual orientation so long as you've had no shady entanglements with the Kremlin. Turned on by truth dealers and justice seekers. Prefer false teeth over false democracy. Doxers, Twitter bots, internet trolls need not apply.

Please Listen Carefully to the Full Menu as Our World Options Have Changed

Press 1 for alternative facts.

Press 2 for an explanation of emollients vs. the emoluments clause.

Press 3 for White House gardening tips from Melania.

Press 4 for denial and anger.

Press 5 for bargaining, depression, acceptance.

Press 6 for lead us not into temptation of nuclear war.

Press 7 if you'd like to purchase a bomb shelter.

Press 8 for racist tweets.

Press 9 if you'd like to hear the Trump administration sing Kanye West's "Wolves."

Or Press 0 if you'd like to speak with Mick Jagger, who can't always get you what you want, but you might find he can sometimes get what you need.

The MAGA Mall of America

Attention shoppers,
at the MAGA Mall of America
lynching ropes and bumpstocks
are available in all stores.

In the center-court area
you can witness
waterboarding demonstrations;
a petting zoo
where you can experience
caged immigrant families
prior to separation
and deportation.

At noon,
Alex Jones will host crisis actors
reenacting
your favorite false-flag mass shootings.

For the convenience
of all shoppers,
a criminal detention center
is located in the basement.
Please report any undocumented workers
or suspicious-looking liberals to mall security.

The former *It's a Small World* attraction,
has been renamed—
It's a White World After All.
Spencer Gifts
is now called Richard Spencer.

Be sure to join us
in the food court
as we build a wall
around El Pollo Loco
to separate all Mexicans
and Mexican food sympathizers
from upstanding American eateries
such as McDonald's, Chick-fil-A,
and KFC.

Food establishments
with questionable allegiances to Mother Liberty—
such as Little Tokyo, Panda Express, and Pita Pit—
will be required to take citizenship tests
before being allowed
to serve the public.

While shopping
at the MAGA Mall of America,
be sure to visit the HUD display
that is manned by no one,
but *is* lavishly furnished.

If you're seeking employment,
walk-in interviews are held daily
for positions within the presidential cabinet.
Please be advised, however,
there is a high turnover rate.
You may find yourself
seeking a new job
within only weeks of your approval.

For your comfort,
the mall is climate controlled
by climate-change deniers.
If you smell something burning
it isn't Cinnabon rolls,
just books.

Barnes and Noble
is now Bombs and Trauma.
L.L. Bean
is now called Lügenpresse.

Be sure to take advantage
of Torture Tuesdays
where a new race, gender, social class,
or member of the LGBTQ community
is brutalized and humiliated.

As is the mall's policy,
alt-right extremists
and those accused of white-collar witness tampering
go unpunished and celebrated,
and receive a 10% discount in all stores.

And don't forget, shoppers,
the MAGA American Girl Store
now carries a new line of T-shirts
emblazoned with the Trump-inspired logo,

Orange is the New Hate.

in the seconds before fingers touch triggers

in the silences
between bombs & gunfire;
from hatred's gutters
to racism's gallows;
amidst tears & tortures,
domestic violence & mass shootings;
over the sounds
of society's psyche
pummeled
into karmic concussion;
locked within the grip
of technology's velocity;
beneath night stars
whose glow
has grown anorexic;
amidst rhythms
of heartbeat jukeboxes
working overtime
to
      pulse,

        pulse,

          pulse—

feel yourself breathing,
               being;

         loving fiercely
       amidst this living war.

Pulse

Pulse of heartbeat.
Pulse of Cyndi Lauper songbeat.
Pulse of lights, pulse of lights.
Pulse of bodies dancing.
Pulse of joy & freedom.
Pulse of heartbeat, pulse of songbeat.
Pulse of clock striking 2 a.m.
Pulse of gunfire.
Pulse of gunfire.
Pulse of brains wondering if that sound
    is part of the song.
Pulse of gunfire, pulse of gunfire.
Pulse of voices yelling, crying, screaming.
Pulse of bodies rushing for safety.
Pulse of bathroom & exit doors swinging open & closed.
Pulse of gunfire echoing through screams.
Pulse of fingers frantically tapping out final texts.
Pulse of sirens, pulse of sirens.
Pulse of bullets searing flesh, shattering bones.
Pulse of bloodshed, pulse of bloodshed.
Pulse of bodies breathing final breaths.
Pulse of bodies feeling final pulse of songs.
Pulse of final breaths & heartbeat songs mixed with blood
    & pulse of sirens.
Pulse of social media blowing up
    with another mass shooting.
Pulse of networks blowing up.
    with another mass shooting.
Pulse of newscasters speaking the names
    of the injured & dead.
Pulse of politicians speaking the names
    of the injured & dead.
Pulse of shock, rage & fear.
Pulse of tears, pulse of tears.
Pulse of anguish & confusion.
Pulse of tears, pulse of tears.
Pulse of time repeating itself.
Pulse of protests, pulse of prayers.

Pulse of protests, pulse of prayers.
Pulse of brains wondering when the next round
of bullets will fly.
Pulse of brains wondering why the next round
of bullets must fly.
Pulse of time repeating itself.
Pulse of protests, pulse of prayers.
Pulse of protests, pulse of prayers.

Quick, turn to the person next to you.
Place two fingers upon their wrist.
Feel the pulse of blood.
Remind yourself you're still alive.

the pound of flesh we must pay

for an ounce of sanity and serenity
as graveyards become far too fertile
with tombstones in this post-atomic, pre-apocalyptic playground
        of paradise lost.

the bright future we strive to build
while climbing out of the deep, ragged pocket
of society's worn-down blues,
countless citizens dancing to the up-tempo
        of the down-low.

the sleep we struggle to find
as insomnia robs our sense of well-being,
nightmares of democracy torn to shreds, mother liberty the second-
hand love
        of alice in asunderland.

hear the voices on all sides of every argument
pump up the volume,   pump up the volume.

if our words are weapons, let them one day
                        be stoned on peace.

A Struggle in the Bones

It's hard to remain calm
when the only seat you're being offered
is in the back of a hearse.

It's a sin when the color of one's skin
presumes automatic guilt,
or that black bodies have hung like strange fruit
from southern trees.

It's impossible to stand idly by when history
continually repeats itself—

a broken record stuck in an ugly groove
of racial brutality.

Imagine, if you will,
spending a lifetime believing
you have the right to remain silent.

That you've been born
only to feel the struggle in your bones,

that you're not worth your very next breath.

When one is continually forced
to close their soul
into a fist,
expect some kind of fight—

be it peaceful

or riot.

Side Effects

Side effects may include bone fractures, hair loss. Unmappable and unconquerable sadness.

Dizziness of dynamism. Diminished well-being. Optimism may experience difficulties in achieving orgasm.

Visual, aural, and tactile hallucinations have been known to occur. Heart may become hacked, held for ransom.

Your shadow may assume the shape of a smoking gun. Additional side effects may include acne, crying spells.

Bone marrow transformed into dead sparrows. Any and all butterflies in your stomach may flap wings, create inner

hurricanes, tornadoes. Un tic-toc timelines of once stable quantum systems, alternative facts generated throughout

the brain. Ringing in ears, loss of smell. Your very next breath may file for Chapter 11 bankruptcy.

Allergic reactions have been known to occur when mixing casual conversation with politics.

You may become thin-skinned, susceptible to rage. Especially with matters concerning race, gender, climate

change, and FBI investigations. Suppression of the body's ability to generate open-mindedness may lead to overeating

and Fox News binge watching. Innovation, fresh ideas, new approaches to life have been known to experience flatulence.

Infrequent side effects may include mouth and anus reversed, so all you do is talk shit, and shit talk.

When mixed with blackmail and highly dubious foreign dignitaries, benevolence has been known to become an

embezzler, money launderer, backstabber. Skin clammy with
selfishness, pustules on politeness, infected equanimity.

Please see your doctor if you experience cruelty for more than
72 hours. Fatal side effects may include Russian collusion,

supporting terrorist organizations such as Neo-Nazis and the KKK.
Other serious events may include

anaphylactic shock of compassion and sheer intelligence. When
properly used, social media activism is usually well tolerated,

but if it leads to uncontrollable Twitter bullying,
internal bleeding has been known to occur.

Drowsiness, dry mouth. Increased susceptibility to fake-news
infection. Prolonged usage may lead to diminished sight in

your third eye. Inner doors of perception may change their locks;
leave you shut out of your own consciousness.

Muscle spasms, rashes, backaches. The once honeyed milk
of human kindness may leave a fishy taste on your tongue.

Seizures, strokes, problems with memory attention.
Which may cause you to forget all of this come morning.

The Autopsy of Democracy

Upon reviewing
the autopsy of democracy,
will you mention that it died
a slow protracted death?

Will you reveal
that its stomach was riddled
with cruelty,
its intestines marred
with embezzlement,
its esophagus savaged
with lies?

Will you overlook the fact
that its body
committed many racist acts
but was continually found innocent
by a jury of its peers?

Upon reviewing the autopsy of democracy,
ask yourself if the corpse
resembles a black body
swinging from a tree.

Ask yourself if the noose marks
around its neck
will preclude it
from an open casket ceremony.

The Gym
Beyond
Good and Evil
Tendencies

The Gym Beyond Good and Evil Tendencies

Lately,
my brain has been working out
at the gym beyond good and evil tendencies.

Nietzsche is my spotter.

He tells me to bench-press
the weight of the world.

Says eternity is now,
so stop worrying whether or not
I'll lose five pounds by tomorrow.

Or how when boxing demons,
don't become your own bruised monster.

Nietzsche tells me
when the punching bag is still,
that's when the fighting man attacks himself.

Says if I don't know how to chill out,
then I shouldn't linger
in the heated sauna of argument.

Or how one quickly sheds pounds
of arrogance
when standing amongst the deserving people
not admiring themselves in the mirror.

Says a thought or possibility
can shatter one's self more quickly
than a hard-ass Pilates class.

Or how, ultimately, one more loves
one's desire for tight abs
than the tight abs that are desired.

When he's done with me,
Nietzsche wipes away my sweat
with his bushy mustache.

Tells me no absolute truths
are waiting for me
at the juice bar.

Florida Man

Florida man
convicted of strangling common sense.

Florida man
arrested for building a meth lab
in an Applebee's parking lot.

Florida man
tattoos Bozo on his cheek
in order to face
his fear of clowns.

Florida man
apprehended for making a sex tape
with himself
in Taco Bell drive-thru.

Florida man
sentenced to life
for trying to smuggle
the apocalypse across state lines.

Florida man
jailed for performing
botched and unnecessary castration surgery
on Ken doll in Walmart toy aisle.

Florida man
caught cultivating
the world's smallest crop
of marijuana
on the head of a pin
where angels once danced.

Possible Reasons Why El Niño Never Made It to L.A.

Became a lyricist
for an Emo band.

A Vegas river-dancer.

The filling for a shit ton of waterbeds—
everywhere from
San Bernardino to Bangor, Maine.

Smoked too much
legal weed in Colorado,
stalled out
over the Rockies.

Feared the construction
of Trump's wall,
never left Ecuador.

Found Jesus,
built a little church
in El Paso—
Isaiah 45:8, Deuteronomy 11:14—
only preached Bible passages
pertaining to rain.

Became a Palm Desert meth addict,
a Hesperia chicken sexer.

Bought a couple
Willie Nelson records,
learned a few chords on guitar,
hightailed it to Austin.

Got work as a bartender
in the Florida Panhandle.
Made a mean Rusty Nail
and Hurricane;
often got stiffed on tips
for watering down drinks—
never on purpose.

Hitched a ride
to Berkeley;
became an absurd Dadaist,
invented a new flavor of Jell-O—

Elb-O.

Lost all its money
in a fantasy football pool,

tricked for a while
at a Barstow truck stop,

caught a nasty disease,
got cured,

then became a priest:
never molested young boys,
only puddled up at their feet.

Drummed for Spinal Tap;
spontaneously combusted
into a badass firestorm
while playing Bakersfield.

Got bogged down
in a lengthy court trial
over a secretly recorded sex tape
involving a ménage-à-trois
with Hulk Hogan & Kim Kardashian.

Donated its services
to Africa's water crisis.

Became a Nogales snake milker,
a Savannah, Georgia cow inseminator.

A short-order cook
at a Mexicali diner—
adored the *hiss-pop-spit*
of bacon on the grill,
shed a tear or two
whenever a jukebox song
wailed the word 'flood.'

Underwent a sex reassignment surgery,
became a sunny day.

Had an identity crisis—
became a breeze,
a bulldozer,
then a butterfly
fluttering off innocuously
into the outer reaches
of invisibility.

Became an Escondido water slide tester,
a Humboldt County serial killer.

Hooked up with a hot-blooded,
wide-hipped tropical storm off Cuba:
fathered a brood of chubby-cheeked,
sparkle-eyed raindrops.

Whenever its ill-weathered wife
whips the seas into tsunamis,
spins winds into hurricanes,
El Niño figures it should gather up the children,
head back to L.A.—

just like the news stations promised.

Superhero/Villain Names for My Self-Defeating Behaviors

Tantrum Man

Captain Passive

Buzzkill Catcher

Vibe Canceller

Psychic Hider

Overspending Sapien

Mixed Message Mentalist

Agent Ambivalence

Commander Late-Night Fast Food Run

Vapid Vulture

Ungodly Nap Monster

Phobophobophobia

Freakishly Fiendish Forget To Do Your To-Do List

Couch Crasher (aka: Gym Avoider, aka: Bubastasis,
aka: Lex Lovehandle)

Procrastinatorsaurus

Dr. Don't

Just a Few of My Childhood Misunderstandings

That seahorses were horses with gills and good posture.

That Superman's crotch bulge was due to rocks in his shorts.

That Transylvania was really Pennsylvania, only with vampires.

That "making love" meant creating something extra special for your mom in art class.

That giving someone the middle finger meant chopping off your own finger and giving it to someone that really pissed you off.

That people shopped naked in strip malls.

That when girls complained about periods, they were super upset about their punctuation.

That every step I took involved the risk of encountering cartoon quicksand.

How to Approach Your Inner Child When It's Wearing Headphones

1) Wear a Sigmund Freud rubber mask.

2) Approach calmly, carefully, your emotional baggage not too heavily packed.

3) Mouth words like "symbiotic," "cooperative," and "reconciliation."

4) Don't wave your arms about. You'll send mixed messages— that you either want to strike your inner child or play a rousing game of tetherball.

5) If the Sigmund Freud rubber mask doesn't work, try Scooby Doo, Goku, or Betty Boop. Definitely not Jabba the Hutt.

6) Wear your own headphones, ignore your inner child.

7) When your inner child isn't looking, plug into its mix.

8) Listen deeply. Explore the sounds of all things wonderful and wounded.

9) Should your inner child ask you to dance, strip away all self-consciousness, and move. The only one watching is you.

10) Should 1 thru 9 fail—here; try this tetherball.

A World of Things

Things we've said under our breath.
Things people have said with their last dying breath.
Things that drive people to drink.
Things that made Jesus think, "Maybe I'm in the wrong line
   of business…"
Things you can only find in Detroit. Things that make you
   jump for joy.
Things that make people jump from the Golden Gate Bridge.
Things you get stuck between your teeth.
Things you've stuck in your ear, up your nose, or
   up your butt.
Things that change from ugly to beautiful.
Things that frighten you. Things that enliven you.
Things to help raise your credit score. Things to help lower
   your cholesterol.
Things organisms have done to adapt.
Things that make certain men become priests.
Things that make certain women wrestle alligators.
Things serial killers think about.
Things you find in a dead man's pockets. Things you find
   in your own pockets.
Things named after Greek Gods. Things people have done
   in the name of God.
Things that cause acne. Things that cause cancer.
Things to consider before having a baby.
Things to consider before joining the French Foreign Legion.
Things you'd do if you had wings.
Things you'd do if you had the Green Lantern's power ring.
Things to help clear out your aura. Things to help clear out
   your orifices.
Things you should always buy generic.
Things you've always wanted to know but were afraid to ask.
Things people have done while under the influence of love.

Things people have done while under the influence of drugs.
Things that make you go "Hmmm…"
Things you see when staring up at the clouds.
Things your pets do when you're not around.
Things you can smoke. Things you can recycle.
Things behind the sun.
Things to make your car run better.
Things you find on the side of the road.
Things you find washed up on the beach.
Things you build. Things you compete for.
Things you do when you're alone in your room.
Things you can burn. Things you can save.
Things to say to get a girl wet.
Things to say to get a guy hard.
Things to say to get kicked off jury duty.
Things you can carry. Things you can hide.
Things that decay. Things that rejuvenate.
Things you put into compost piles.
Things that live under your skin.
Things you find around Jim Morrison's grave.
Things your doctor won't tell you.
Things your parents won't tell you.
Things your lover won't tell you.
Things your best friend won't tell you.
Things the major corporations won't tell you.
Things the government won't tell you.

Will *never* tell you.

Maybe

Maybe I should count sheep. Maybe get out of bed,
go for a walk.

Maybe I should do laundry. Wash the dishes, clean
the toilet.

Maybe I should get on the computer: Google search
fun facts about the human body or discover which animal—
dogs or cats—have better night vision.

Maybe I should figure out how to get rich quick. Or how
to correctly balance my checkbook. Or get my chakras balanced.

Maybe I should count more sheep. Pop an Advil PM.

*Or maybe just yell for my downstairs neighbor to turn down his stereo so I
can finally get some sleep.*

Maybe I should sort my junk drawer. Lint roll all my black clothes.

Maybe learn more about politics, world religions, threatened
indigenous cultures.

Maybe I should go shoplifting at an all-night Ralphs.
Then return everything I steal.

Maybe I should go back to school, get a Masters. Or learn
to be the master of my destiny.

Maybe I should take my filthy car to an all-night
self-service carwash.

*Or maybe just hop in my dirty car
and run over my downstairs neighbor's stereo
so I can finally get some sleep.*

Maybe I should figure out a way to end wars
and world hunger.

Maybe learn why asparagus makes my pee smell weird.
Or why orange juice and other things taste strange
after brushing my teeth.

Maybe I should clean and polish my shoes. Or buy
a new pair: ones that are both fashionable and functional.

Maybe figure out why my family is so *dys*functional.

Maybe I should make a list of all the movies I've seen,
or a list of famous musicians who were also killers,
or inventors who were killed by their own inventions.

Maybe I should get outdoors more. Try kayaking, tobogganing, or
hammer throwing.

Or maybe just throw a hammer through my downstairs neighbor's window.

Maybe I should drive the Autobahn. Or experience weightlessness.

Maybe I should learn a new language, visit more art galleries,
perform more community service work.

Maybe I should grow an herb garden. Get a tattoo
or body piercing.

Maybe figure out why humans do things like fart,
blink, blush, hiccup, or straight up lie.
Maybe I should get in touch with my dark side.
Become best friends with a mortician, or serial killer.

Or maybe just hire a serial killer to eliminate
my downstairs neighbor.

Maybe I should stop saying Yes when I really mean No.
Or rehearsing arguments in my head I never end up having.

Maybe I should try something that scares me daily.
Or maybe start with something safer: collect stamps,
tea towels, or Beanie Babies.

Maybe it's time I accept the idea of having a family
and baby.

Maybe I should write my will. Finally write the great American
novel.

Maybe I should alphabetize my books by authors, titles, better yet
by ideas.

Maybe I should finally read *House of Leaves*, *Ulysses*,
or *The Art of War*.

After that: go to war with my downstairs neighbor.

Butt Dialing
for Danny Baker

I get a call from a buddy of mine. He tells me how I butt-dialed
him the other day. Says he listened to the entire eleven minute and
fifty-seven second call without once interrupting. He just sat there
quietly, wondering if, at some point, I'd reveal a salacious piece of
gossip. Or maybe, my buddy feared, he'd overhear something far
darker—me involved in a car crash or falling victim to someone's
road rage. Instead, my buddy says, the butt dial was just a swimmy
sounding eleven minutes and fifty-seven seconds of me engaged
in my usual morning activities, saying things like: *Venti, please*, and
Where the hell did I put my keys now?! and loudly humming along with
my car radio blaring the NPR *Morning Edition* theme song.

After my buddy and I are off the phone, I start wondering what
other people my butt might be dialing behind my back. But instead
of relaying the garbled and swimmy sounds of my day-to-day
activities, I'm suddenly gripped with the fear my butt hasn't only
been dialing, it's also been doing all the talking—to family, friends,
and business associates.

I can see it now.

Soon the hate calls will start pouring in, everyone telling me how
I've become such a flaky son-of-a-bitch. How I've become *So L.A.*,
making all these plans and promises then blowing them off. To
everyone, I'll be saying: *You gotta believe me! I didn't call you! It was
my good-for-nothing ass!* To which they'll all reply: *Yeah, right! Leave
your ass out of it! You're the one that's the ASS!*

Next thing I know, my girlfriend will be telling me how much she
likes my ass. At first, I'll be foolish enough to believe she means
she likes the shape of it, how it feels. But then I'll wake up one
night, find her next to me in bed, *on the phone*, my butt having
dialed her, the two of them talking all hot and heavy and low; my
ass murmuring all the sweet nothings I have such a hard time
conveying in the real world.

My ass has probably been dialing all kinds of people without my knowledge: signing up for aerobics classes, scheduling massages, therapy appointments, buttock augmentation surgery, BDSM sessions, phoning sex chat lines.

Soon the bills will start flooding in from all the missed appointments with the head therapist, Swedish massage therapist, butt doctor, dominatrix, and gym. Weird 1-900 charges will start popping up on phone bills. To everyone, I'll be saying: *You gotta believe me! I didn't call you! I didn't sign up for your head-shrinking, fat-burning, muscle-building, butt-toning, smut-talking, bondage session! It was my lowdown, good-for-nothing ass!*

I have no idea what I've done to make my ass so passive-aggressive. Maybe I've sat on it too much, or too little. Haven't exercised it enough. Haven't soaped it up enough in the shower, haven't bought the right type of clothes to highlight its features.

And what about all the butt beatings I've received through the years: when my old man would smack my ass with a hand or belt for my every behavioral misstep. Or the time in 3rd grade when my teacher beat my butt with an inch-thick wood paddle in front of the class when I wouldn't stop drumming "Wipe Out" on my desk. Or in 5th grade when the class bully kicked my ass for my non-ironic Spam T-shirt.

And what about all the things I stuck up my butt when I was a kid: my toy submarine, the neighbor girl's Barbie doll head, my old man's car keys, all those dried beans I should've been using for kindergarten art projects.

What about all the times I used the word *ass* in vain. Said things like: *Suck ass. Dumb ass. Drag ass. Thumb up your ass. Head up your ass. Hard ass. Half ass. Your ass is grass. What's up his ass? Talking outta your ass!*

Real fast, I better do something special for my ass: take it out for a nice long hike, buy it a new pair of form-fitting jeans, soap it up extra good in the shower. At least sit down with it, have a good long talk. Apologize for how insensitive I've been. How, for so many years, I've been such a pain in the ass to my ass. Then I'll promise my ass that if I ever receive a butt dial—no matter how muddled or mundane it may sound—I'll listen to the entire call. Especially if it's my own butt dialing. Maybe I'll overhear a car crash, or a potential murder in progress. If so, I'll yell for help. Dial 9-1-1.

Who knows?

The life I save may even be my own.

The Summer of South Jersey House Parties

Riding a rabid twist on a blackout boogie down,
it was the summer of South Jersey house parties.

Bong blasts and tequila shots
till cross-eyed;
one too many Long Island Iced Teas
mixed with
one too many long looks
at someone else's girlfriend—
the recipe for a fistfight.

Those parties:

beer-bellied, tobacco-chewing Pineys
boozing elbow to elbow
with diner waitresses, divorcees,
ex-cons, slutty ex-cheerleaders
& clean-cut, recent high-school grads like me,
getting our first real taste
of the raw-boned wild side.

Always a muscle car or two
parked on dirt lawns.

Tangled in those backseats:

long, lean girls
pregnant with reckless desires;
muscled thugs,
black cats stalking their psyches—
sweat-soaked savage lovers
hopped up on black beauties & Black Sabbath,
bone knocking to *Sabotage*,
windows fogged.

Those parties:

every Saturday night,
we of itchy minds and feet,

hearts hurling bricks
through glass walls of inhibitions,
danced gangly limbs akimbo
inside cigarette & water stain-walled shotgun shacks.

Juiced on Jack,
and the DJ's playlist,
we brushed up against the opposite sex
like sticks rubbing together,
sparking fires—

burning hips,
burning hopes,
burning the hours away
to Cheap Trick, Blondie, Springsteen.

Kisses
tasted of Stoli,
Binaca, Marlboro.

Handjobs, blowjobs,
illicit affairs
in shadowy backyards;
the moon-washed night air
wreathed any wrongdoings
in hibiscus and cricket symphonies.

Our collective exuberance,
synonymous with our fashion sense:

badass bomber jackets;
brightly colored short shorts;
frilly bras stuffed with tissues & socks;
Led Zep T-shirts, sleeves hacked off.

That summer of South Jersey house parties—

some, like me,
would soon go off to college.
Still others:
to trade school or the military.

The rest remained stuck in town,
drunk and stumbling
from one house party to the next;

dancing to Skynyrd, Stevie Wonder,
Donna Summer—

Last dance, last chance for love

A Man, a Megaphone, a Lonely Room

Anyone who is allergic to intimacy or has maintained a love/hate relationship with Mr. Rogers.

Those who've used a weedwhacker to eliminate the dark and overgrown areas of a once-clean conscience.

Anyone who has mistakenly said "premature ejaculation" instead of "premeditated adoration."

Those who've painted their mirrors black. Whose metal hip screws have set off security alarms at CVS.

All whose paychecks have evaporated like the most recent L.A. rains.

Women who've considered shaving their heads and joining the convent. Men who've considered shaving their heads when going bald.

Anyone who has played a six-string while using a live grenade as a guitar slide.

Those who've recently made a new friend or connection online or standing on line, waiting to get into a supermarket or hospital emergency room.

For those dying on the streets, in homes, hospices, or remote villages a world away.

For anyone whose heart is breaking. For anyone whose heart is healing.

Everything is Radiant
Between the Hates

Everything Is Radiant Between the Hates

Days boobytrapped with animosity,
reeking of gunpowder's acrid bite—

when
the bass-heavy beat
of police brutality
makes it so you can't breathe,
and kids begin the new school year
with face masks and bulletproof backpacks;

when
homegrown terrorists
keep getting younger,
and bullet speech
grows louder;

when
those who perish
from shootings,
beatings, lynchings,
overdose, and disease
are reduced to
body-bag hashtags
on social media.

So heavy these days
when chaos holds sway,
and pallbearers bear the weight
of still another coffin
across the worn, cobbled streets of our eyes.

In between it all—

moments of grace:

a kind word,
a shared kiss,
offering a child

tinder-stick phrases
such as *please* and *thank-you*
to illuminate
their journey forward.

Here,
contentment is revealed,

everything is radiant
between the hates.

Blueprint for a Better World

Cars will run
on poems, prayers,
and the courage
of Sojourner Truth.

All guns
and assault weapons
transformed
into high-powered Pez dispensers.
The NRA
has changed its name
to the NEA.

Birdhouses
will be built
atop gravestones.
Gardens planted
in the hearts of the lonely.
Lightning bug halos
for everyone.

Earthquakes, tornadoes,
and tsunamis
take anger-management classes.
Dogs and cats
call a lasting truce.
Rainbows
donate their colors
to the severely depressed.

There'll be
a cross fertilization
of dreams, free speech,
and the almighty dollar—
a new currency we can exchange
through liplock.

In utopia's dance hall,
we'll be non-stop
bump and grind music;
an exhilarating hectic electric
flowing through our veins.
When we touch radios,
light bulbs, and guitar amps,
they'll come alive.

There'll be
dependable road signs
along the highways
of our minds.
Clarity and foresight
will be dressed
in easy-to-spot, polka-dot blazers,
placed at every
entrance and exit ramp
to ambivalence and obscurity.

All mirrors
will reflect
our inner beauty;
our sweet-cheeked,
moon-eyed,
push-button perfection.

The very air we breathe
will never be used against us
in the court of life.

All our burdens,
and regrets;
paragraphs of scattered thoughts.
We'll edit one another down
until we're
naked and radiant.

Our glowing bones,
the blueprint
for a better world.

To-Do List

Live more.
Laugh more.
Have more sex.
Explode orgasmic mind juice
into active imagination.

Make necklaces
of fiery L.A. sunsets,
ones you can
give away
at freeway exit ramps,
Skid Row,
or battered women's shelters.

Write more.
Sing more.
Play more guitar.

Leave all
mental & metaphysical doors
wide open.
Allow poetic muses
to pay unannounced visits
at all hours;
even if
they show up drunk
or with muddy feet.

Exercise more.
Walk the dog more.
Adopt dog logic—
where everything
is pure instinct,
pure expression.

Clean out your closet.
Give away
what you don't need.
Give away
what you think you need.

Especially
what you think you need.

Breathe more.
Meditate more.

Paint
your darkest thoughts
baby blue.
The rest:
a blazing
Van Gogh yellow.

Drink more water.
Eat more fruits
and vegetables.

Don't lie.
Don't cheat.
Don't be deceitful.

Basically,
don't be an asshole.

And remember:
All the sins
your father
passed along to you,
don't accept them
as your own.
Instead,
donate them
to Buffalo Exchange
to be resold
as edgy
fashion accessories.

Spend more time
in nature.
Speak
to birds, trees.
Be the tree.
Imagine that kind
of stillness,
and patience.

Be
stillness and patience.

Brush your teeth
at least
twice a day.
Don't
chew your food
with your mouth open.

Don't condemn.
Don't kill.
Don't approach this life
as war.

And if you need
to carry a bomb,
let it be filled
with grace & generosity.

Explode beauty.
Explode color.
Explode joy.

Be a bliss terrorist.

Get more sleep.
Get more informed.
Learn to be
your own best friend.
Learn to be happy
with what you have,
and don't have.

Especially with
what you don't have.

Trade in
all your sad goodbyes
for newly reconditioned
hellos.

Develop a binding theory
of compatibility.
Know that love
doesn't trap you,
it sets you free.

Don't waste your time.
Don't waste
other people's time.

Don't mistake
silence
for annihilation
or submission.

Make
your inner light,
living light.
Don't
build mausoleums
behind your eyes.

Phone your parents more.

Send more letters to friends—
through U.S. Mail,
not email.

Clean out
the junk mail
from your
email inbox.

Greet each day
with a smile.

Make your
eyebrows kazoos;
teeth, keyboards;
chin, a bass drum;
so that when you speak
you're a one-man band.

And finally,
build yourself
a Louis Armstrong gun.
Its ammo:
soulful vocals,
and trumpet wails.

Every shot:
the sounds
of a wonderful world.

An Elegy, Uplift We

Like an elegy born from the heartstrings,
humming, thrumming; raging through blood,
praying through blood, can you hear our song?
An elegy, uplift we.

For our paradise trampled, untended,
stuffed into an envelope marked return-to-sender.
An elegy, uplift we.

For our paradise hacked, fracked,
its freedom flag lowered to perpetual half-mast.
An elegy, uplift we.

Paradise bombed, globally warmed.
Bullied & berated, thrown under the bus.
Paradise bruised & misused,
left stumbling, mumbling at the edge of sanity.
Paradise raped, robbed, running scared.
Segregated, deteriorated,
labeled DOA,
surrounded by pallbearers.

For our paradise lost,
for a paradise gained,
where tranquility is just a kiss away,
an elegy, uplift we.

For those banging at the door
of fearful night, an elegy, lift it up.

For those following body maps
to dark, dangerous destinations,
up the up.

For the residents at the insomniac motel,
lift it.

For the mothers & fathers whose children
are stricken by disease, lift it higher.

Breathe life into the child,
breathe life into the mother & father,
breathe vitality into the sleepwalker,
breathe vivacity into you & me—
an elegy, uplift we.

All the prisoners for their torturers,
all the torturers for their victims,
lift it.

When our mirrored reflections hiss, "kill,"
utter, "malice be mine," promise, "heads will roll,"
lift it.

In the name of the Bothered, Stunned,
& Tortured Ghost, let an elegy uplift.

Up it higher for decimated Mother Nature;
her polluted waters, her sickened fish, fauna & fowl.

Up the up higher for the mercenary heart,
how it continues beating
through even the most savage days—

when walls of fists rise all around us,
when touch equals attack,
when common decency falls victim to greed & brutality,
when soul-deaf defeatists search out
Armageddon's melody
in the sounds of breaking hearts & bones.
For a sweeter, more harmonious music in our ears,
an elegy, uplift we.

Uplift an elegy
for our peace, promise & reason,
our suffering, sadness & rage.

Uplift an elegy
for all our perfections, all the mistakes we've made,
all the right & wrong things we've said,
for what was never said, what we should've said.

Uplift an elegy
for an E-pluribus you & me—
a true unification, regardless of race, religion,
or sexual orientation.

Deep in the gut, our elegies are born.
Every day, we uproot that groove bone of grace.
We shake that bone. We shake that bone.
We bring our songs. We sing our songs. We be our songs.

We dance until our chains shake away.

In the Bird Hospital

In the bird hospital
intricate machines
beep & whir
chirp & blurb
steady rhythms.

Doctors administer
regular doses
of tenacity & stability,
patience & dedication.

A wing healed here,
a pain dissolved
& transformed
into a nest there.

In the bird hospital
tiny bones
are mended into song.

Flight is brought back to life.

In My City of Words

In My City of Words

Black cats
cross my path;
slip-slide
through puddles
of hymns, laments
& sapphic verse.

The letters on street signs,
freeway entrance
& exit-ramp signs
rearrange into
haikus, couplets & cantos.

Billboard messages
co-mingle;
create ballads, sestinas,
epic & erotic poetry.

Free birds sing free verse.

Cars crash into one another;
bring new meaning
to slam poetry.

when your tongue gets pulled over for speeding

speak politely to the officer.

make nouns
sound like muzzled revolutions;

adjectives,
puffs of air through trees.

make adverbs
beige's handmaiden.

once you've been cleared,
floor it;

drive full-throated,
singing, screaming, speeding
straight into verbs'
gleaming, streaming gold.

Verb the Noun for Better Societal Sounds

Cathedral our chaos.
Butterfly our gravity.
Hurdy-gurdy our worries.
Pop-Tart our heavy hearts.
Elegy our police baton'ed knees.
Funny bone our tombstones.
Megaphone our quiet hopes.
Matlock our padlocks.
Keyhole our blind spots.
Emily Dickinson our pandemic.
French kiss our peaceful protests.
Mistletoe our every woe.
Candy cane our soured grace.
Lucky penny our failing democracy.
Dog park Barr's nameless army.
Cheetah our entropy.
Maserati our anti-racist engine.
Cardamom our curfew'ed streets.
Mozart our every breath.

Homonym Hymn

No need to murder
a murder of crows,
or sing a song
of sing-sing too loud.

No need to billy club
a dance club,
or cruelly stalk
a beanstalk.

Don't turn your forearms
into firearms, and fire holes
into a fire.

Don't work a graveyard shift
at the graveyard,
or rock out
with rocks in your pocket.

It'll only make your guitar frets fret.

Mama's Home-Cooked Words of Wisdom

My mama never allowed me to borrow the devil's compass when going on a trip.

Said never give your phone number to strange shadows. Never sleep in the middle of the road, or use a porcupine as a pillow.

My mama never allowed me to speak too loudly in the libraries of church light.

Washed my mouth out with the moon if I forgot how to sing the stars.

Wouldn't let me keep broken mirrors as pets,
or turn my heart into a stone to strike others with hate.

She said never throw out your bubbliness with the old bubble-bath water.

My mama never allowed me to ingest disinfectants as a way to kill the germs in my body.

Love You Vs. Lick Me

The typewriter in my heart
is battered and befuddled,
but well meaning.

The U is stuck,
the comma is in a coma,
and the ! ran off with the ?
to join the circus.

The O thinks it's an I
and sometimes an E.

The V crossdresses as a C.

The E's alternate personality is a K,
and the Y had letter reassignment surgery
to become an M.

So whenever
I try to type the words "Love You"
it always comes out

"Lick Me."

So Go the Quiet Passings of Many Unhistorical Moments

Picasso often made love in a papier-mâché house
with a violin-tongued mistress
whose passionate moans were a wildfire.

In that room of her own,
Virginia Woolf engaged in pillow fights
with the silence,
and non-linear make-out sessions
with the moon.

During his second term as president,
Lincoln built a tiny log cabin in his mind.
In it lived his mother who had died when he was nine.

Even after Lincoln's death,
his mother lived on in that cabin—

sewing, singing along with sparrows,
playing lullabies for Lincoln's ghost
on her steel-drum teeth.

A Lengthy Introduction to a Very Short Poem

The poem
you're about to hear,
I first discovered
an early version of it
in the back of a cross-country Greyhound bus,
just outside Kansas City.

It
was hanging with two hippie girls,
Opal and Sierra—
starry-eyed waifs,
beads and feathers woven in their hair,
peasant dresses reeking of weed and patchouli.

The poem
you'll soon hear
was ready to abandon
its MFA degree
and two years of PhD coursework,
all to follow Opal and Sierra
as they followed
the Grateful Dead on their 1993 tour.

Another thing
regarding the poem
you're about to hear—
while it clocks in
at a mere seventeen seconds,
I feel there's so much more
to say about it:

Its muses are elusive.
Its fingerprint barely a whisper.

Its DNA
has never been discovered
on any computer,
in any writing journal,
or publication.

The poem
was inspired
by all the thoughts
that have awoken me
in the middle of the night;
ones I promised myself I'd jot down,
then promptly fell back asleep
and forgot.

The poem
is gender-neutral,
highly political,
anti-gun,
anti-hate,
anti-rape,
anti-discrimination.

Doesn't contain
a whiff of erotica,
but it does allude to a time
when it was involved in a brief,
but highly contentious relationship
with a seemingly naive sonnet
that turned out to be
a toxic, vindictive,
extremely manipulative,
and remorseless sociopath,
that burned the poem you'll soon hear
with a stun gun,
walloped it with a shovel, shot it,
rolled it into a carpet,
and tossed it into the Pacific.

It did, however,
manage to survive
with only a few minor scrapes to its title,
and a slight limp in its first stanza.

The poem
you'll soon hear
is a lexicon of second chances—

it once saved a child
from a burning building,
an old man from a mugging,
and a young woman
from being abducted.

To truly understand
and appreciate the poem
you should populate its interior
with artwork
inspired by the seven wonders
of your most ancient emotions.

Build a window
into its west-facing wall.

Every day for a year,
observe the sunset.
Upon witnessing the 365th,
strip off your clothes,
paint your body
with all the colors that best describe
your credit score at the time.

Then run naked through the streets.

If you're arrested,
burned with a stun gun,
walloped with a shovel,
shot,
rolled into a carpet,
and tossed into the Pacific—

then and only then
will you fully comprehend
the poem's deepest meaning.

The poem
you'll soon hear
yearns to bare its soul,
reveal its flaws—

its
whines, mopes,
and placid form.
Its erratic meter,
mixed metaphors,
and awkward alliteration.

It doesn't have a face
for wearing hats,
or a voice for radio.

No talent
for horse whispering,
or finding its keys and phone
in the dark.

Gets cold in the summer,
warm in the winter.

Doesn't know its up from down,
its left from right.

Attends auspicious literary events
with dog hair
covering its most scholarly thoughts.

Still,
the poem you're about to hear
knows to say thank you
when offered kind words,
or constructive criticism
in a writers' workshop.

Never burps or farts
in public.

Always wipes its feet
before entering your ear
to reveal its innermost feelings.

In a nutshell,
the poem you'll soon hear
only seeks your love, trust,
and attention.

All it asks
is that you listen
to its words,
the silences
between those words,
and the silences
between the silences.

And now,
the poem...

An Abridged History of Lips

An Abridged History of Lips

Abe Lincoln's lips
are stone pillars
on which rest the sun-bleached bones
of democracy.

Angelina Jolie's lips
are durable flotation devices
to be used in the event of a flood.

Stephen Hawking's lips
are a schematic drawing of the cosmos.

The egotist's lips are pride
never fully swallowed.

The homeless vet's lips
are mental shrapnel wounds
never fully healed.

And your lips
are parentheses
between which exist
desires—

so clarified & kissable.

Closer

It's sort of respect for another person and have that person respect you...
You wear a mask, they wear a mask, you protect each other.

— Dr. *Anthony Fauci*

Would you dare?

Maybe.

At less than arm's-length?

We'll see.

What about now?

What's that? I can't understand you.

Should I take off my face mask?

Perhaps.

What about now? Would you dare?

Only if you think so.

What if I know so?

Know what?

That I want to tell you I love you.

But you can say that at more than arm's length.

But isn't closer better?

As in this close?

Closer.

Closer?

Yeah, you haven't forgotten what that feels like, have you?

A Better Use for My Shadow

On your tongue I taste
the electricity
& pandemonium,
of coming rains.

Oh, love—
you're a booty shaker,
a blossom maker.

When my body
leaves this earth
tie my shadow
between two trees,

make me
your dream hammock.

For You

Guns, knives,
and bombs
become lavish bouquets
of blood-red roses.

For you,
Death takes a week off work.

Cemeteries become libraries
where you can read deep
into the souls of the lost.

For you,
the Four Horsemen of the Apocalypse
give up war, famine, pestilence,
and the rest,
to form a barbershop quartet.

For you,
congregations of alliteration
sing sonorous soliloquies
of spiritualization.

For you,
warships become tulips,
which become my lips,
kissing you.

Sex

Some have sex with bombs to procreate death & destruction.

Some have sex with saxophones to give birth to the blues.

Some have sex with machines to seek harmonization with automation.

Some have sex with the theory of relativity when they need a good mind fuck.

Some have sex with libraries for the intelligent conversation.

Some have sex with redactions when they're feeling secretive.

Some have sex with skyrockets in flight to achieve "Afternoon Delight."

Some have sex with statues to obtain absolute stillness.

Some have sex with the present moment to give birth to a better tomorrow.

She Wants, Like He Wants, But I...

after Juan Felipe Herrera

She wants a 14K yellow gold Marquise diamond ring,
like he wants a Maserati Alfieri / but
$$I$$
want a storm of sensual symphonies
raining down on my love & me;
our naked bodies tuned to the key of sex major—
rolling, writhing, slipping, sliding;
our limbs touching, tangling—
the two of us becoming one great rock opera of ecstasy & elation.

She wants Louboutin Flame sandals,
like he wants a Fibonacci Pocket watch / but
$$I$$
want DNA deejays to remaster my hips,
blood beats mixed & remixed,
pure swooning, no need for auto-tuning;
a smooth-talking body language
between my love & me—
bumping, grinding, finding absolute bliss
in lust's dark, delicious dance hall.

She wants Italian White Alba Truffle,
like he wants a bottle of 1958
Domaine de la Romanee Conti / but
$$I$$
wanna tickle, lick & fuck my love all day
as honeybees coax smut talk from flower petals,
& carnal gardens give rise to the plump, scrumptious,
hot & juicy cherry of Hell Yeah. I said *Hell Yeah.*

She wants a 55-piece diamond little black dress,
like he wants a 540 Sundancer Speedboat / but

   I

want my love & me to go shot for shot,
chugging down the glorious elixir of euphoria—
partying, prowling, humping, howling,
keeping the universe up all night;
solar systems crooning, spiral galaxies grooving,
until morning arrives,
that bloodshot-eyed sunrise, screaming
at my love & me:

"Get a room already!"

If

If you polish my adam's apple, make a rockband
of my adrenal glands.

If you grease my elbows with your elbow grease,
release all the fibs from my fibula.

If you take the Sisyphus boulders from my shoulders. Deem my
humerus humorous,
my femur a lemur,
my feet a feat of strength.

If you Depeche Mode my lymph nodes,
Spinal Tap my spinal cord,
transform my teeth
into an Exile on Main Street.

If you mercy my molars,
reconstruct my navel into a rave,
Route 66 my esophagus.

If you render my glands grand,
and my hair unhurried—

I'll make my blood vessels your eternal lover.

Something About Our Eyes

There are times when our eyes are more than just eyes.

Like when they bellchime heartshine.

Did I say bells?

I meant soul-mirrors eclipsing sun, reflecting one another's
unclouded inner visions.

Did I mention clouds?

Our eyes are more like colorful rugs not yet pulled out
from beneath us,

flying carpets sailing us to the farthest limits of devotion and back.

Rugs?

How about bookstores & bodegas,
carnivals & harmonic through-lines
singing us from cradle to grave.

Did I say wondrous?

Yes, there are times when our eyes are more than just eyes.

Of Elevator Belly Buttons and Socrates' Single Sock

Just yesterday,
I found one of Socrates' single socks
in my laundry basket.
I hung it from my chipped statue
of introspective questioning.

Whenever I'm at a loss for words
or get tangled in tongue-tied suppositions,
I hear the rattling of the bones, bolts, and rivets
holding me together.

I'm nowhere near enlightenment
when my belly button
only serves as an elevator button
leading me to the basement of primal instincts.

On a lighter note,
the cage that is my body has a lock
you can easily pick with a smile.

When Wilhelm Röntgen Visits the Farm

for Russell Edson

When Wilhelm Röntgen visits the farm
the moon jumps over the cow;
sheep play ping-pong with unstable isotopes;
geese and goats get stoned,
create cathode-ray light shows.

When Wilhelm Röntgen visits the farm
pigs wallow in radioactive baths;
ducks contemplate the phenomena
of spreading oil drops on water;
backhoes harvest the souls of all beings.

The farmer awakens to a fluorescent light
beside him in bed;
he witnesses the X-rayed bones of his wife—
shimmering like tractor headlights in the dark.

When Wilhelm Röntgen visits the farm
rainbows elope with gamma rays;
horses gallop through electrostatic fields;
corn crops spike silky hair,
pierce ears, crank punk rock.

And as
the farmer and his wife—
upon their creaky bed in a drab pre-dawn room—
plow the aged furrows of one another's bodies,
weariness melts away;
visible hearts beat faster, brighter—

everything glows.

Evelyn Everything

The Adoration Parade

In your presence,
my heart shreds itself
to confetti,
becomes
a tickertape celebration.

Our hellos:
pageant floats.

Shared laughter:
marching bands.

Look just outside
the windows of your eyes.

Witness all the tiny pieces
of me
flickering down
around your feet.

And so begins
the adoration parade.

Love Poem for My Young Daughter on Valentine's Day
for Evelyn Everything

You were still
a vague notion
in my mind—
like trying to grapple
with the concept of infinite pi—
until your mother
sent me that first picture
of you,
just moments after your birth.

So radiant.
Eyes closed and serene;
divinity's tiny seed.
Our first year together
was rough—

Old family loops—
my father's rage,
mother's sorrows—
left me untrained
to the music of soothing you.

More attuned
to those rhythms,
your mother
often
consoled you.

With time,
I learned
to embody her song:

perform neat and clean
diaper changes;
rock you back to sleep
after a night terror;
bottles of formula

at the ready
for 2, 4, and 6 a.m. feedings;
every morning,
sing along
with your birdsong burblings.

Certain evenings,
I'd creep into your room,
place a hand
on your sleeping chest
to monitor your breathing.
Your belly's
finely spun rise and fall;
a warm, flesh-bundled hum.

In those moments,
my existence
became a still center point
around which
circled murmured prayers
dedicated to your wellbeing.

With each devotion,
the old ashes of me re-flowered.

In Praise of Beastless Beds

I search beneath your bed
to ensure there are no monsters
bearing the odor of heartbreak;

monsters bearing wicked grins
marred with nightmare-graffitied teeth;

monsters stealing wonder, leaving only wounds.

Before I sail you off to sleep,
I leave you with these words:

Bring me a necklace of moons,
and I'll play you a song on my jukebox heart.

Meet me at the intersection of Grace and Good Fortune.

heart be

heart be lavish / heart be light
heart be legal / heart be lecherous
heart be lendable / heart be leased
heart be lazy / heart be leapfrog
heart be unleper'ed / heart be leopard
heart be learned / heart be labeled

heart be lankiest loudest lambent likable ladybug

Tattoo You

You are the flapjack tattoo

                    on my blackjack.

You are the sweet word tattoo

                    on my bird turd.

Angel Baby

You are lightning spined;
jukebox chakra'd;
your every heartbeat—
novena.

A quiet geography of strength
borders your blood's empire.
An untamable spirit
resides in the wolf-howl altar
behind your eyes.

You are the one
continually rising
from tragedy's ashes.

You are the one
whose prophets of peace
heal the bullet holes
in my shattered thoughts.

Your wings,
you sometimes offer
as spares
to any angel
whose first flight

is a troubled one.

Things About Myself and the World I Will and Won't Explain to My Four-Year-Old Daughter When She's Older

First, drugs.
I'll definitely discuss drugs.
But I probably won't mention the time
I snorted heroin
in a dingy McArthur Park hotel room.
Or the times
I tripped on mescaline, mushrooms,
ecstasy, LSD—
laughing my ass off,
witnessing the walls and people's faces melting,
time traveling,
telepathically communicating
with animals, insects, trees.

What I will explain to my daughter
is how drugs
can be both dangerous and alluring.
How one can get so easily hooked
on the rush, the giddiness, the floating away.
How there are days
when all people want to do is float away.
I'll teach my daughter
how things like art, music, and poetry
can offer a much purer sense
of floating way.

I'll discuss how poetry
has so greatly influenced my life.

That said,
I probably won't mention the time
I was scheduled to do a featured reading,
yet wound up in the hospital that day.
Won't reveal how
when I realized I'd be in the hospital

much longer than I'd expected,
yanked the IV from my arm
when the nurse wasn't around;
scrambled into my clothes,
seized a cotton ball to clot
the unnerving pulse of my blood spraying the walls;
snuck out of the hospital,
hailed a taxi, sped off to my feature.

And *rocked* it.

I'll teach my daughter
the importance of empathy,
compassion, consideration.

That said,
I probably won't mention the time
I was blind drunk at my brother's wedding;
skied naked,
received a summons from the Wisconsin water police—
even after I'd slurringly tried convincing them
that if they didn't ticket me
I'd take them back to L.A.,
make them big TV stars—

a river version of *CHiPs*.

I'll figure out
how to describe to my daughter
the utter remorse and humiliation
I experienced as a teenager
upon being nabbed by store security
in a K-Mart parking lot
after I'd shoplifted the soundtrack
to *Saturday Night Fever*.
I didn't even want the damned cassette.
All I'd wanted
was for my parents to stop fighting,
and not get divorced.

I'll do my best
to prepare my daughter
for ages 13 through 19;
how those years will be
one great big life-affirming,
soul-crushing rush of proms,
relationships, acne, breakups, and all the rest.

I may even find the appropriate moment
to offer a cautionary tale or two:
how my dumb-assed teenaged buddies and I
would drive drunk,
spin doughnuts on people's pristine lawns,
jam potatoes in car tailpipes,
steal road signs—

all because we had no idea
how to express our reckless and random
hormone-fueled emotions
any other way.

Then I'll play for my daughter
The Who's "Baba O'Riley."
We'll dance through the house,
celebrating and commiserating
in the joys and sorrows of those coming years;
loudly singing along as The Who wails:

"Teenage wasteland. It's only teenage wasteland."

I'll teach my daughter
honesty, justice, determination.
Will support her in maintaining
a positive body image.
I'll confess how in high school
I used an ice cube
and Zippo-heated dirty sewing needle
to pierce my ear,
how it became an infected, swollen mess.
Suffered through shots and antibiotics
for well over a week,

all for the sake of wanting to fit in
because my dumb-ass buddies kept telling me
I'd look much cooler
if my ear were pierced.

I'll point out to my daughter
the importance of never letting anybody,
including herself,
bend up her aura,
reshape her inner light
into an unflattering shine.
How certain mistakes
can never be completely undone,
but in the best possible circumstances,
their DNA can be altered
to embody subtle forms of forgiveness and grace.

How our every breath and heartbeat
have the potential
to compose verses on air—
sonnets of love when it's freshly baked,
glorious stories of coyote-blooded magic
sending us roaming wild-toothed,
and full-moon footed
into the dense forests of the absolutely alive.

I will warn my daughter
that this is a world where people can hurt and heal.
That there exists the goodness of strangers,
and the absolute cruelty
of those we've considered friends.
How the bitterness and anger
we sometimes experience
is no city for permanent refuge.

In the face of it all,
I will teach my daughter
to wear her name proudly.
Let it be a cradled murmur in the ear.
Bubble & luck. An Attila the Hun of fun.
A get-out-of-jail-free card,
and her own star on Hollywood Boulevard.

May the mere mention
of my daughter's name
be a cathedral of sweet talk.
Hummingbird flutter.
And on her most troubled days,
may my daughter's name
be the tears that travel in reverse
to unstain her cheeks,
and brighten her sad, sad eyes.

About the Author

Pushcart Prize-nominated poet Rich Ferguson has shared the stage with Patti Smith, Wanda Coleman, Moby, and other esteemed poets and musicians. Ferguson has been selected by the National Beat Poetry Foundation, Inc. (NBPF), to serve as the State of California Beat Poet Laureate (Sept. 2020 to Sept. 2022). He is a featured performer in the film, *What About Me?* featuring Michael Stipe, Michael Franti, k.d. lang, and others.

His poetry and award-winning spoken-word music videos have been widely anthologized, and he was a winner in *Opium* Magazine's Literary Death Match, L.A. He is the author of the poetry collection, *8th& Agony* (Punk Hostage Press), and the novel, *New Jersey Me* (Rare Bird Books).

rich-ferguson.com

Acknowledgements

Huge and heartfelt thanks to all the editors for including my work in your publications. It is a true honor to be a part of your fine literary family.

"Things About Myself and the World..." – *The Rumpus*

"Things About Myself and the World..." – Winner of the *Deanna Tulley Multimedia Contest* 2018 (Video directed by Victor Guzman)

"In the Gomorrah of Glamour and Gimme All You Can" – Honorable Mention / *Deanna Tulley Multimedia Contest*, 2019 (Video directed by Chris Burdick)

"A Lengthy Introduction to a Very Short Poem" – *Suitcase of Chrysanthemums* (great weather for media, 2018)

"Phantom Poem Syndrome" – *Before Passing* (great weather for MEDIA, 2015)

"Please Listen Carefully to the Full Menu..." – *Maintenant 13* (Three Rooms Press, editors Peter Carlaftes & Kat Georges)

"Deep in the Bowels of a One-Note Downtown" and "Love Poem for My Young Daughter on Valentine's Day" – *Cultural Weekly* (edited by Alexis Rhone Fancher)

"She" – *Sensitive Skin*

"A Worry Bead, A Blessing" and "When Called in For Questioning" - *Coiled Serpent: Poets Arising from the Cultural Quakes & Shifts in Los Angeles* (Tia Chucha Press)

"Seven Cards" – *Connotation* (edited by Karen Stefano)

"Just Moments After Eternity's Musicians…," "Side Effects," and "When Wilhelm Röntgen Visits the Farm" – *Brazen: A Painting & Poetry Collection* (edited by Keith Martin)

"In the Gomorrah of Glamour and Gimme All You Can" – *Edgar Allan Poet #3* (edited by Apryl Skies & Danny Baker)

"Mama's Home-Cooked Words of Wisdom" – Susan Hayden's *Library Girl*

"What Was Said at the Reunion of Deathbed Wishes" – *Maintenant 14 Anthology* (Three Rooms Press, 2020)

"So Go the Quiet Passings of Many Unhistorical Moments" – *Escape Wheel* (great weather for MEDIA anthology, 2020)

"Post-Apocalypse To-Do List" and "Another Day in L.A." – Greg Olear's *Prevail*

"Summer of South Jersey House Parties" – Aris Janagian's *Artifactuals*

"Wanting," "certain days feel so heavy," "The Autopsy of Democracy," "What My Inner Executioner Has Told Me On Many Sleepless Nights" – *Arteidolia* – a collaboration with visual artist Kathleen Reichelt

A Million Moons of Gratitude and More

Once the pandemic set in and it became clear I wouldn't be able to tour this book as I'd done in the past with previous releases, I began to think differently about how to gather blurbs for this collection. Perhaps I overdid it a bit. Still, I consciously sought words from the people I'd most want to read and perform at my book release party, had we been able to gather face-to-face. So here it is, instead, my literary party in the written-word flesh. These blurbs were not only gathered to celebrate the release of this collection, but to also celebrate the work of my fellow writers and artists, and to thank them for being so eager and willing to support me during these troubled times when it would've been so easy and understandable if they'd simply said they didn't have the time nor attention to do so.

A million moons of gratitude and more to the following blurbers: J. Ryan Stradal, Jonathan Evison, Rob Roberge, Gayle Brandeis, Greg Olear, Kim Shuck, Alexis Rhone Fancher, Jane Ormerod, Richard Modiano, Richard Loranger, Andrew Tonkovich, Lisa Alvarez, Bill Mohr, Iris Berry, Susan Hayden, S.A. Griffin, Milo Martin, Paul Richmond, Kathi Flood, Kelli Allen, Stephanie Barbé Hammer, Elizabeth Hazen, Conney Williams, Alexandra Umlas, Pam Ward, Briana Muñoz, Paul Corman Roberts, Dave Bonta, Kate Belew, and Aimée Keeble. Also, a huge and heartfelt thanks to Heather Woodbury for writing the forward to this collection.

A million moons of gratitude and more to Debbie Tosun Kilday at the National Beat Poetry Foundation, Inc. (while I can think of so many other candidates equally worthy of the title, I thank you for honoring me as California Beat Poet Laureate). Another round of thanks to Quentin Ring and the Gang at Beyond Baroque (I can't wait to get back there and perform some day!). Blessings to Kim Shuck (Poet Laureate of S.F.) for her wise words, guidance, and allowing me a sacred online space to read.

A million moons of gratitude and more to folks like Jane Ormerod, Thomas Fucaloro, Peter Carlaftes and Kat Georges for publishing my work. Thanks to Thomas Zandegiacomo Del Bel and the fine folks at ZEBRA Poetry Film Festival. Shoutout to Jamie Catto, Duncan Bridgeman, Bob Holman, Kathleen Reichelt, Kim McMillon

Monica Valdés, Butch Norton & Joe Kara, Tom Rossi, Jeremy Toback, Herb Graham Jr., Mark Wilkinson, Chris Burdick, Cat Gwynn, Alexis Rhone Fancher, Andrei Rozen, Rosanna Gamson, Brad Listi, Gina Frangello, Nicelle Davis, The Pondwater Crew, Bill Burnett, Suzy Williams, Gerry Fialka, Eric Carter, Liz Foster, Tyson Cornell, Seth Fischer, Andrew Bush, Josh Haden, Frédéric Iriarte, Ritt Henn, Joshua Corwin, and all the other folks that have allowed me to collaborate with them in some form or another during the pandemic, and throughout the years.

A million moons of gratitude and more to those who've offered support and inspiration during the pandemic and throughout the years: my mother and father, my brother Dr. Bob, Crystal Lane Swift, Milo Martin, Chris Camacho, James Morrison, Wayne Reynolds, Brendan Schallert, Keith Martin, Karen Ford, Sid Stebel (R.I.P.), Dave & Jim & Dot, Katherine Williams & Richard Garcia, Julie Kodama, Jimmy Jazz, all the good folks at Squaw Valley Writers Retreat, Liz Newstat (Chevalier's Books), Charles Hauther (Skylight Books), Chris Tannahill, Jerry the Priest, A.K. Toney, Gwen Goodkin, Tony Saavedra, Jessica Apoorva Larsen, Tania Van Tuinen, Eva Požar, S.B. Stokes, Merle Brezianu, Dulce Stein, Jonathan Campbell, Alisandra Del Nero, Amelie Frank, and so many more.

A million moons of gratitude and more to Patrick O'Neil for patiently and persistently battling the technological glitch-demons to create my website.

Another million moons of gratitude and more to Joanna C. Valente for the stunning cover photo.

Still another million moons of gratitude and more to Christianne Ray for her friendship, keen P.R. skills, steadfast support of my work, our creative collaboration on the video "Everything is Radiant Between the Hates," and for helping to guide me through the dark and treacherous forests of self-promotion where I inevitably find myself a bit lost.

A million moons of gratitude and more to Eric Morago at Moon Tide Press for believing in my work and me. Thanks to Dania Ayah Alkhouli for her behind-the-scenes assistance. Also, a nod to some of my fellow Moon Tide authors: Jennifer Bradpiece,

Kelly Gray, Peggy Dobreer, Kathryn DeLancellotti, Gustavo Hernandez, and John Brantingham. It's an honor and pleasure to be literary stablemates with each and every one of you.

Last, but certainly not least, a million moons of gratitude, and oh so many more, to my Evelyn Everything. For you, my dear daughter, I cannot offer enough moons to rival the brightness you bring into my life.

Patrons

Moon Tide Press would like to thank the following people for their support in helping publish the finest poetry from the Southern California region. To sign up as a patron, visit www.moontidepress.com or send an email to publisher@moontidepress.com.

Anonymous
Robin Axworthy
Conner Brenner
Bill Cushing
Susan Davis
Peggy Dobreer
Dennis Gowans
Alexis Rhone Fancher
HanaLena Fennel
Half Off Books & Brad T. Cox
Donna Hilbert
Jim & Vicky Hoggatt
Michael Kramer
Ron Koertge & Bianca Richards
Ray & Christi Lacoste
Zachary & Tammy Locklin
Lincoln McElwee
David McIntire
José Enrique Medina
Michael Miller & Rachanee Srisavasdi
Michelle & Robert Miller
Ronny & Richard Morago
Terri Niccum
Andrew November
Jennifer Smith
Andrew Turner
Rex Wilder
Mariano Zaro

Also Available from Moon Tide Press

When the Pain Starts: Poetry as Sequential Art, Alan Passman (2020)
This Place Could Be Haunted If I Didn't Believe in Love, Lincoln McElwee(2020)
Impossible Thirst, Kathryn de Lancellotti (2020)
Lullabies for End Times, Jennifer Bradpiece (2020)
Crabgrass World, Robin Axworthy (2020)
Contortionist Tongue, Dania Ayah Alkhouli (2020)
The only thing that makes sense is to grow, Scott Ferry (2020)
Dead Letter Box, Terri Niccum (2019)
Tea and Subtitles: Selected Poems 1999-2019, Michael Miller (2019)
At the Table of the Unknown, Alexandra Umlas (2019)
The Book of Rabbits, Vince Trimboli (2019)
Everything I Write Is a Love Song to the World, David McIntire (2019)
Letters to the Leader, HanaLena Fennel (2019)
Darwin's Garden, Lee Rossi (2019)
Dark Ink: A Poetry Anthology Inspired by Horror (2018)
Drop and Dazzle, Peggy Dobreer (2018)
Junkie Wife, Alexis Rhone Fancher (2018)
The Moon, My Lover, My Mother, & the Dog, Daniel McGinn (2018)
Lullaby of Teeth: An Anthology of Southern California Poetry (2017)
Angels in Seven, Michael Miller (2016)
A Likely Story, Robbi Nester (2014)
Embers on the Stairs, Ruth Bavetta (2014)
The Green of Sunset, John Brantingham (2013)
The Savagery of Bone, Timothy Matthew Perez (2013)
The Silence of Doorways, Sharon Venezio (2013)
Cosmos: An Anthology of Southern California Poetry (2012)
Straws and Shadows, Irena Praitis (2012)
In the Lake of Your Bones, Peggy Dobreer (2012)
I Was Building Up to Something, Susan Davis (2011)
Hopeless Cases, Michael Kramer (2011)
One World, Gail Newman (2011)
What We Ache For, Eric Morago (2010)
Now and Then, Lee Mallory (2009)
Pop Art: An Anthology of Southern California Poetry (2009)
In the Heaven of Never Before, Carine Topal (2008)
A Wild Region, Kate Buckley (2008)
Carving in Bone: An Anthology of Orange County Poetry (2007)

Kindness from a Dark God, Ben Trigg (2007)
A Thin Strand of Lights, Ricki Mandeville (2006)
Sleepyhead Assassins, Mindy Nettifee (2006)
Tide Pools: An Anthology of Orange County Poetry (2006)
Lost American Nights: Lyrics & Poems, Michael Ubaldini (2006)

Even More Praise for
Everything Is Radiant Between the Hates...

Ferguson lays down the prayer carpet, wipes off his muddy boots and caterwauls with a sharp and timeless tongue laced with timely beatitudes of oily angel wings and the sparkling teeth of gargoyles.

— Milo Martin, author of *Poems for the Utopian Nihilist*

If you don't believe words have power, then you haven't read or heard these words.

— Paul Richmond, US National Beat Poet Laureate 2019-2020, owner of Human Error Publishing

Reading *Everything Is Radiant Between the Hates* is like dropping a mic directly into Rich Ferguson's brain; he is that transparent and true, rapid-fire and sincere.

— Kathi Flood, visual artist and poet

These poems are the sheet music for songs we have all been waiting to feel reverberate in our own newly-worthy throats.

— Kelli Allen, author of *Banjo's Inside Coyote,
Imagine Not Drowning, Otherwise Soft White Ash*

Bold, generous and self-deprecating, Ferguson's work challenges readers to accept grief and dare — despite it, *because* of it — to dream of glorious things.

— Stephanie Barbé Hammer, author of *How Formal?* and
T*he Puppet Turners of Narrow Interior*

Rich Ferguson's poems jump off the page, the words singing in your ears as you read, images dancing, energy pulsing in every line.

— Elizabeth Hazen, author of *Girls Like Us*

Ferguson's lyricism shows that a *teenage wasteland* can transform into something radiant, even *lightning bug halos.*

— Conney Williams, poet/actor/activist, author of
Leaves of Spilled Spirit and *Blues Red Soul Falsetto*

In Rich Ferguson's extraordinary new collection of poetry, energy and lush language propel the reader into intersections of humor, desire, politics, Los Angeles, and the deep love we feel for our children.

— Alexandra Umlas, author of *At the Table of the Unknown*

Rich Ferguson's *Everything Is Radiant Between the Hates* grabs the metaphor by the neck and squeezes.

— Pam Ward, author of *Want Some Get Some* and *Bad Girls Burn Slow*

Ferguson includes thought-provoking but gentle poetry on the political. Each stanza, within, flows like a jazz chord, in true beat-poet form.

— Briana Muñoz, Author of *Loose Lips* (Prickly Pear Publishing 2019)

It's a difficult thing to be a poet of the people, and a very different but equally difficult thing to be a poet of the Cosmos. Rich Ferguson is that rare writer.

— Paul Corman Roberts, author of *Bone Moon Palace* (Nomadic Press 2021)

Rich Ferguson brings beat poetry into the post-truth era, challenging the forces of chaos and apocalypse with a big-hearted and deeply American vision of balance.

— Dave Bonta, poetry filmmaker and author of *Ice Mountain: An Elegy*

Rich Ferguson takes us on a dreamy poetic adventure beginning with sleepless nights, the dental records of long-lost moons, and a coyote orchestra.

— Kate Belew, poet

A loud and lawless work, truths spoken from a mouth that has seen much, suffered much, danced much, loved much.

— Aimée Keeble, poet, creator of The Beat Goes On